OUR HEAVENLY FATHER

Faith and Life Series

Third Edition

BOOK ONE

Ignatius Press, San Francisco
Catholics United for the Faith, Steubenville, Ohio

Nihil Obstat: Reverend James M. Dunfee
                  Censor Librorum
Imprimatur: +Most Reverend R. Daniel Conlon
                  Bishop of Steubenville

Director of the First Edition: The late Rev. Msgr. Eugene Kevane, Ph.D.
Assistant Director and the General Editor of the First Edition: Barbara M. Nacelewicz
First Edition Writer: Daria Sockey
Revision Writer: Colette Ellis, M.A.

Catholics United for the Faith, Inc. and Ignatius Press gratefully acknowledge the guidance and assistance of the late Reverend Monsignor Eugene Kevane, former Director of the Pontifical Catechetical Institute, Diocese of Arlington, Virginia, in the production of the First Edition of this series. The First Edition intended to implement the authentic approach in Catholic catechesis given to the Church through documents of the Holy See and in particular the Conference of Joseph Cardinal Ratzinger on "Sources and Transmission of Faith." The Revised Edition and Third Edition continue this commitment by drawing upon the *Catechism of the Catholic Church* (Libreria Editrice Vaticana, © 1994, 1997).

Excerpts from *The Penny Catechism* (Prow Books, Kenosha, WI, 1970), and from the Pius X Catechism of Christian Doctrine (Center for Family Catechetics, 1980). Catholics United for the Faith and Ignatius Press are grateful for permission to reprint copyrighted material.

Unless otherwise noted, Scripture quotations have been taken from the Revised Standard Version of the Holy Bible, Second Catholic Edition, © 2006. The Revised Standard Version of the Holy Bible: the Old Testament, © 1952, 2006; the Apocrypha, © 1957, 2006; the New Testament, © 1946, 2006; the Catholic Edition of the Old Testament, incorporating the Apocrypha, © 1966, 2006, the Catholic Edition of the New Testament, © 1965, 2006 by the Division of Christian Education of the National Council of the Churches of Christ in the United States of America. All rights reserved.

Excerpts from the English translation of The Roman Missal © 2010, International Committee on English in the Liturgy, Inc. All rights reserved.

The Subcommittee on the Catechism, United States Conference of Catholic Bishops, has found this catechetical text to be in conformity with the *Catechism of the Catholic Church*.

Contents

A Note to Parents

Dear Parents,

    The *Faith and Life* series was originally published in 1984. The book you hold in your hands is one of over 4.6 million books sold since then. From the beginning, the series was intended to provide schools, parishes, and families with the catechetical tools and essential elements of Catholic doctrine pivotal in the formation of young Catholics.

    While the doctrines and Tradition of the Church remain essentially unchanged, as time has passed the editors have provided additional teaching tools that enrich the series and make it even more accessible to all types of students. Since its introduction, the series has seen the addition of activity books, teacher's manuals, numerous online resources, scriptural quotations, and correlations with the *Catechism of the Catholic Church*. Additionally, this edition has been updated to incorporate the new translations of the Roman Missal introduced into the Mass during Advent 2011.

    In this first grade student text, *Our Heavenly Father*, you will find that emphasis has been given to the scriptural basis of our Faith in accord with Sacred Tradition. Every chapter opens with a Scripture passage, and important verses supplement the text where relevant. Each chapter closes with questions and answers based on Church teaching as found in the *Catechism of the Catholic Church*. Vocabulary words are indicated in bold type and in the Words to Know sections. Their definitions are found in the glossary. Common Catholic prayers are also taught in the lessons, and presented at the end of the book.

    It is important to realize that, as parents, you are the primary educators of your child. Your active participation in your child's religious education is highly encouraged by the Church. As a family, you are the first witnesses of God's love to your child. If you provide a model of Catholic living at home, if as a family you participate in the sacramental life of the Church, and if you pray and attend Mass together, your child is more likely to take to heart the lessons he will learn in religion class. Family discussions of current events with a healthy religious perspective will allow your child to grow up with a better understanding of the world around him, and more importantly, help him to be a true Catholic and follower of Christ in the midst of it. As stated in the *General Directory for Catechesis*, "family catechesis precedes . . . accompanies and enriches all forms of catechesis" (GDC, 226; Congregation for the Clergy, 1998). Providing your child with a strong Catholic identity at an early age, while not ensuring a lifetime of devotion, will certainly prepare him for the challenge of becoming a faithful Catholic adult.

    We encourage you to use the *Our Heavenly Father* student text, along with its resources, to assist you in the task of sharing the Good News with which you have been entrusted. More information and resources can be found at www.faithandlifeseries.com.

    We sincerely hope that this series will provide parents, catechists, and teachers with the assistance they need in the task of evangelizing young people.

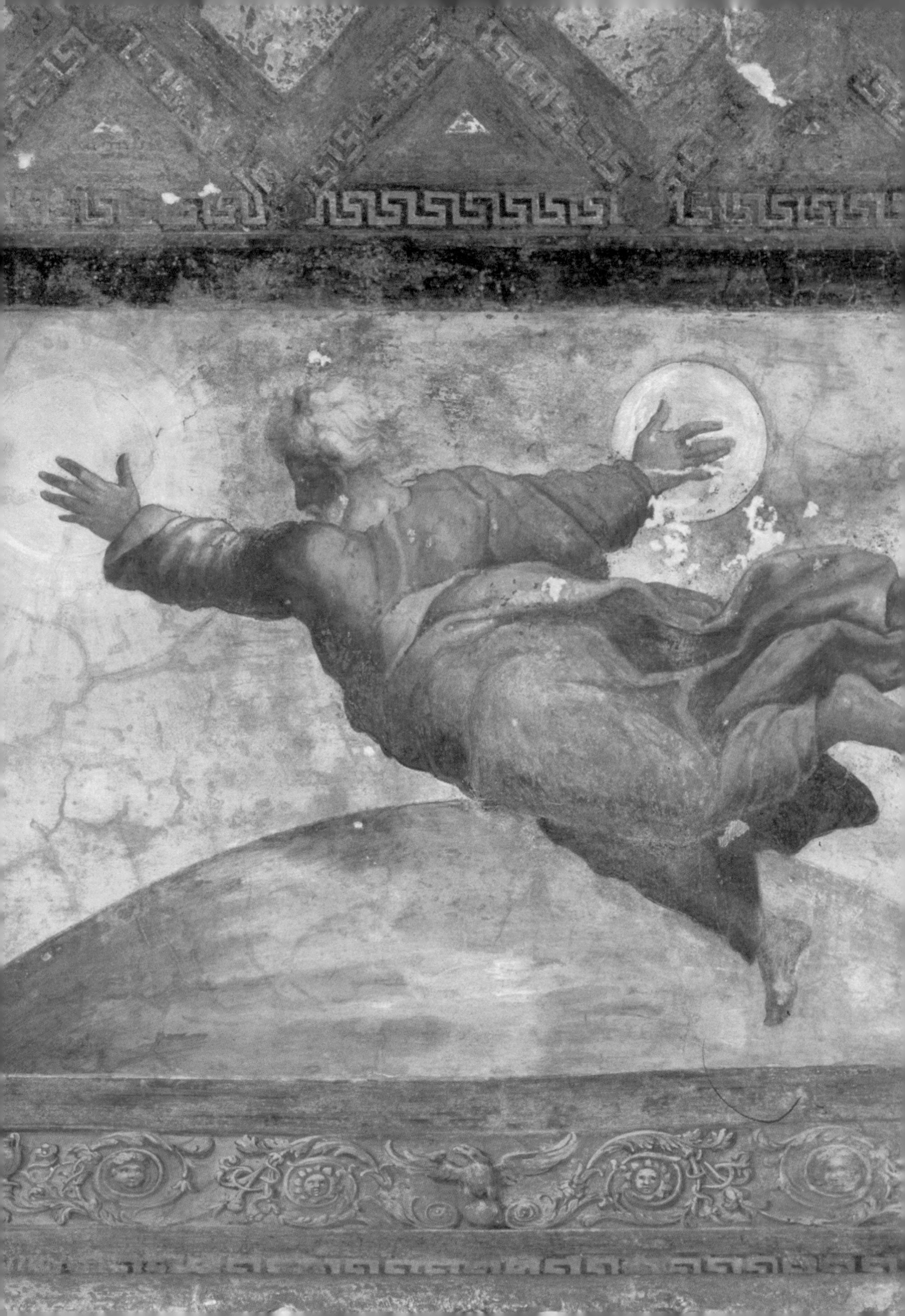

1   God Is Our Father

"Behold, I have graven you
on the palms of my hands."
                    Isaiah 49:16

Did you know that you have a Father who is
in Heaven? He is your Father. He is your parents'
Father. He is your grandparents' Father. He is the
Father of all of us. He is God.

God is the One Who made us. God made the
world we live in, too. He made flowers, vegetables,
trees, and animals. God made the sun and the stars
and the big, blue sky. He also made rivers and lakes
and oceans, and everything there is.

Why did God make you? God made you because
He loves you very much. Because God loves you,
He watches over you day and night. He does this
by giving you all the things you need. So the food
we eat, and the things we need to make clothes and
houses, all come from God.

God gives you your family, the people who take

care of you, and all the people you love. God makes many things you like, things like warm sunshine, icy snow, and lots of water in which to swim. He also did not forget to make all the animals that make us happy.

How good our Father is! We should give thanks to God for all these gifts, like this:

Thank You, God, for everything!

When you talk to God, He always hears what you say. That is what **prayer** is—talking with God. God wants us to pray to Him. He loves us and wants us to talk to Him about everything.

God wants you to call Him "Father." So we can remember, He even gave us a prayer called the **Our Father**. It begins this way:

"Our Father, Who art in Heaven..."

Words to Know:

prayer   Our Father

Q. 1   *Who made you?*
God made me (CCC 355).

Q. 2   *Why is God called Father?*
God is called Father because He is the
Creator of the world (CCC 238).

Q. 3   *How does God our Father show His love?*
God our Father shows His love by caring
for His children (CCC 239).

We Pray:

OUR FATHER

Our Father, Who art in Heaven, hallowed be Thy
Name; Thy Kingdom come; Thy will be done on
earth as it is in Heaven. Give us this day our daily
bread, and forgive us our trespasses, as we forgive
those who trespass against us; and lead us not into
temptation, but deliver us from evil. *Amen.*

2   Heaven Is Our Home

"…no eye has seen, nor ear heard, nor the
heart of man conceived, what God has
prepared for those who love him."

1 Corinthians 2:9

In the last chapter, we learned that God is our
Father. In the prayer that Jesus taught us, we say
"Our Father who *art* in Heaven." The word art is an
old-fashioned word. It means *are*. So we see that
God our Father is in **Heaven**.

Do you know what Heaven is? Heaven is God's
home and a place of perfect happiness. It will never
end.

Now close your eyes and think of the most
beautiful place you have ever seen. Think of the best
time you ever had. Think of the things you love to do
and the things that taste best. Well, Heaven is better
than all of that!

Now comes the best part: God wants you to come

to live with Him in Heaven someday. In Heaven you will be happy with God forever and ever. And in Heaven, no one is ever sad or hurt or crying. You can pray:

Thank You, God, my Father, for wanting to share Your home with me. Amen

Words to Know:

Heaven   Sign of the Cross

Q. 4   *What is Heaven?*
Heaven is God's home and a place of perfect happiness (CCC 326, 1024).

We Pray:

THE SIGN OF THE CROSS

When we talk to our Father in Heaven, we often begin and end our prayer with:

In the Name of the Father, and of the Son, and of the Holy Spirit. *Amen.*

While we say the words, we make a big cross by touching with our right hand first our forehead, then our chest, our left shoulder, and finally our right shoulder.

3   God Watches Over Everything

"For you love all things that exist..."
Wisdom 11:24

God is everywhere, not just in Heaven. You cannot see God, but He looks after you all the time, wherever you are.

God is all powerful. He can do anything! No one is stronger than God.

God knows *everything*. He knows what every fish and bug and bird is doing right now. He knows what you are doing and even what you are thinking.

God created all things—every single thing! To **create** is to make something out of nothing. Once there was only God: there was no light, no outer space, no earth, no water, nothing but God. Then God said, "Let there be light! Let there be sky! Let there be land and water!" And there it was, just like that, just the way God said.

God created **angels** too. Angels are like God in one way because they do not have bodies. They are invisible spirits.

All the angels were very good when God created them. Then some of the angels turned away from God. That means they chose to become bad; they became **devils**. The good angels stayed with God to be His helpers.

God is all good. Everything about God is good. He takes care of all that He has made. He takes care of the stars and the planets. He takes care of the animals and the trees. Above all, God takes care of you and loves you very much.

Words to Know:

create   angels   devils

Q. 5   *Where is God?*
God is in Heaven, on earth, and in every place (CCC 2794–96).

Q. 6   *Can God do all things?*
Yes, God can do all things (CCC 268–69).

Q. 7   *Does God know all things?*
Yes, God knows all things, even our thoughts (CCC 305).

Q. 8   *Why is God called "the Creator of Heaven and earth"?*
God is called the Creator of Heaven and earth because He made all things out of nothing (CCC 290–91).

Q. 9   *What are angels?*
Angels are invisible spirits. They are God's helpers (CCC 328–30).

4 God's Special Gifts

"For he will give his angels charge of you
to guard you in all your ways."
Psalms 91:11

Once upon a time, not long ago, there was *no you*! Then God decided He wanted very much to have a boy or a girl like you. So He made you. He gave you life inside your mother. You were very tiny. Then, when the right time came, you were born.

God gave you a **body** so that you can do all sorts of things. Your body can run and it can climb and jump and play. And God gave you eyes that are looking at this book right now, and ears that can listen to a story, or music, or any sound. And you can taste ice cream with your tongue, touch puppies with your fingers, and smell cookies with your nose. God gave you all these wonderful things.

God also gave you a **soul**, a very important and special thing. The soul is the part of you that makes you live. It is invisible, but real. Because you have a soul, you can think and love and choose what to do.

You can laugh at something funny. You can understand a story, too, and you can tell what is right and what is wrong—all because you have a soul. And your soul is the part of you that will never die.

Your body and your soul are very special to God. He gave you a **guardian angel** to help you take care of them. Your angel is always looking after you because he is your very own angel. Your guardian angel helps you to do what is right because he is your friend.

Your guardian angel helps you get to Heaven where God wants you to be with Him forever. You must be very good to go to Heaven. You must know, love, and serve God in this world. God wants you to study hard and pray often. He wants you to receive the Sacraments of Penance and Holy Communion. He also wants you to be an obedient and loving child.

Here is a prayer you can say:

Thank You, dear Father, for life and for the other wonderful gifts You have given me. *Amen*.

Words to Know:

body   soul   guardian angel

Q. 10 *What makes you a human person?*
I am a human person because I have a body and a soul (CCC 362–65).

Q. 11 *Will your soul ever die?*
No, my body will die, but my soul will live forever (CCC 366).

Q. 12 *What must you do to gain the happiness of Heaven?*
To gain the happiness of Heaven I must know, love, and serve God in this world (CCC 202; Mk 12:30).

Q. 13 *Does everyone have a guardian angel?*
Yes, everyone has a guardian angel who is with him all the time (CCC 336).

We Pray:

PRAYER TO MY GUARDIAN ANGEL

Angel of God, my guardian dear,
To whom God's love commits me here,
Ever this day be at my side,
To light and guard, to rule and guide. *Amen.*

5   Adam and Eve

"Then God said, 'Let us make man in
our image, after our likeness; and let them
have dominion...over all the earth...'"

Genesis 1:26

Long, long ago, God made the world. Then He
made the first man and the first woman. They were
called **Adam** and **Eve**.

God gave them a beautiful place in which to
live. It was called the Garden of Eden. There were
trees in the garden with good things on them to eat.
Adam and Eve had everything they wanted. They
were never sick or hurt, and they never had to die.
All the animals were their friends, too.

God also gave Adam and Eve another very
special gift. He gave them the gift of sharing His very
own life. With God's life in their souls, Adam and
Eve could know, love, and serve God. And they could
live with Him forever.

God gives this gift to us, too. The life of God in our souls is called **grace**. Grace makes us able to go to Heaven. It makes us children of God.

Adam and Eve were our first parents because all the people of the world came from them.

Words to Know:

Adam   Eve   grace

Q. 14 *Who were the first man and woman?*
Adam and Eve were the first man and woman (CCC 375).

Q. 15 *What was the special gift God gave Adam and Eve in the Garden of Eden?*
The special gift that God gave Adam and Eve was grace, God's life in their souls (CCC 54, 356, 375).

26

6   A Sad Story

"...sin came into the world through
one man and death through sin..."
Romans 5:12

One day, God gave Adam and Eve a test. He told them never to eat the fruit from one of the trees in the garden. God wanted Adam and Eve to **obey** His command, and for a while they did.

But one day, the devil pretended he was a snake and came into the garden. He told Eve to go ahead and try some of the forbidden fruit from the tree. He said it would make her just as smart as God.

Eve knew that she should obey God, but she listened to the devil instead. She ate the fruit. Then she gave some to Adam and he ate it too. This was the very first **sin**. Sin is saying no to God. That is what Adam and Eve did.

So Adam and Eve had to leave the lovely garden. Now they had to work hard for their food. And now they had to die someday. Worst of all, Adam and Eve lost the gift of grace. Without God's life in their souls, Adam and Eve could not go to Heaven. The gates of Heaven were closed. Adam and Eve were very sad and very sorry.

Adam and Eve lost God's gift of grace for all of us too. Now everyone is born with the sin of Adam and Eve on his soul. It is called **Original Sin**.

God felt sorry for Adam and Eve because He still loved them. He felt sorry for all the people who would come after them too. So He made them a **promise**. A promise is when you say you are going to do something and really mean it. God promised to send a **Savior**. The Savior would win back God's grace for us and open the gates of Heaven again.

Words to Know:

obey   sin   Original Sin   promise   Savior

Q. 16 *What is sin?*
Sin is saying no to God. It is a failure to love God. It is any evil thing that we choose to do, think, or say (CCC 1849, 1850).

Q. 17 *Who committed the first sin on earth?*
Adam and Eve, our first parents, committed the first sin on earth (CCC 399, 416).

Q. 18 *What happened to Adam and Eve because of this sin?*
Because of this sin, Adam and Eve lost grace, Heaven, and life in the Garden of Eden (Gen 3:23–24; CCC 390).

Q. 19 *What has happened to us because of Adam and Eve's sin?*
Because of Adam and Eve's sin, we are born with Original Sin and without grace. We inherit their punishment (CCC 418).

"I will look with favor on the faithful in the land, that they may dwell with me . . ."

(Psalms 101:6)

7   A Time of Waiting

"I will look with favor on the faithful in
the land, that they may dwell with me..."
Psalms 101:6

God promised to send a Savior. But the Savior
did not come right away. The people had to wait for
years and years. While they waited, some of them
learned to love and obey God.

Noah was one of those people. Others did not
obey God and fell into sinful ways. But Noah always
did what God asked of him; he was **obedient**. Since
Noah and his sons were the only people on earth who
loved God, He decided to begin the earth again with
his family. But first He would wash the earth clean of
sin with a flood.

God told Noah to build an **ark**. The ark was a
big boat. Then God told Noah to fill the ark with all
the different kinds of animals. After all the animals
were in the boat, God told Noah and his family to
climb inside and close the door very tightly. Once

they were inside, it began to rain very hard. Soon a flood covered the whole earth. Because Noah and his family obeyed God, they were safe and dry and cozy inside the ark.

Later, there was another man who loved and served God. His name was **Abraham**. He had **faith** in God, a gift that makes us able to believe all that God tells us. Abraham was always obedient to God, even when it was difficult. God promised to make of Abraham a great nation. From these people the Savior would be born. Some of Abraham's descendants are still among us today. They are the people we now call the Jewish people.

Words to Know:

Noah   obedient   ark   Abraham   faith

Q. 20 *What did some people do as they waited for the Savior?*
Some people believed in God and obeyed Him so they would be ready for the Savior (CCC 58–64).

8   Getting Ready For the Savior

"The law of your mouth is better to me than
thousands of gold and silver pieces."
Psalms 119:72

Many more years passed. The descendants of
Abraham were still waiting for the Savior. God did
not forget His promise. He sent many **prophets** to the
Jewish people. Prophets were holy men who prepared
people for the coming of the Savior, Jesus Christ.

Moses was the first prophet. Moses was very

important because God gave him the Ten Commandments.

The **Ten Commandments** are God's Laws for every one of us. These Laws help us to know how God wants us to live. When people obeyed God's Laws, they were preparing for the coming of the Savior.

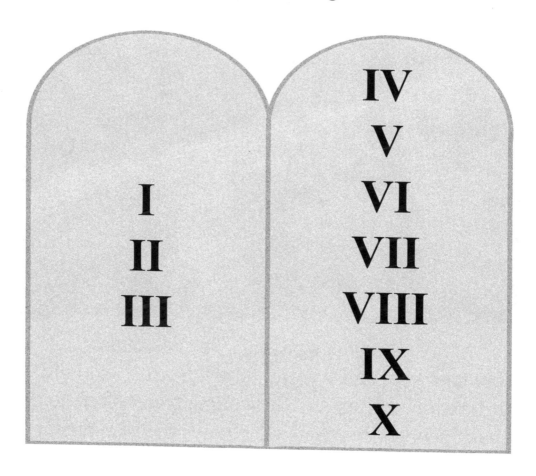

Then when it was almost time for the Savior to come, God sent the last prophet of the Old Testament. He was **Saint John the Baptist**. Saint John was the cousin of Jesus. He lived and prayed in the desert. He told people to be sorry for their sins. Saint John baptized people if they were sorry for their sins. This baptism was not the Sacrament of Baptism, but it helped people to prepare for the Savior. Saint John told the people that the Savior would come very soon.

Words to Know:

prophets   Moses   Ten Commandments

Saint John the Baptist

Q. 21   *What are the Ten Commandments of God?* The Ten Commandments of God are the moral law that God gave to Moses on Mount Sinai (CCC 2056).

9   Mary Hears Some Wonderful News

"Behold, I am the handmaid of the Lord;
let it be to me according to your word."
Luke 1:38

Finally, the time came for the Savior to come into the world. There was one last thing to get ready.

There was a girl named Mary. **Mary** lived in a town called **Nazareth**. God loved her so much that He gave her the gift of grace that Adam had lost for everyone else. Mary was free from Original Sin from the very first moment of her life. She loved God so much that in her whole life she never committed even one single sin. Everything she did made God happy.

When Mary grew up, God sent the angel **Gabriel** to visit her. Gabriel told Mary some wonderful news. He said that God wanted her to be the Mother of His Son, the promised Savior.

Mary trusted that God knew what was best. So Mary said, "I am God's servant. Let it be done to me as you say." That is how Mary became the Mother of **Jesus**.

God's very own Son came down from Heaven to live with us. God also chose a special man named **Joseph** to be Mary's husband and to take care of Jesus. Since God is the real father of Jesus, we call Joseph the foster-father of Jesus.

Words to Know:

Mary   Nazareth   Gabriel   Jesus   Joseph

Q. 22 *Who is the Mother of Jesus, the Savior?*
Mary is the Mother of Jesus, the Savior (CCC 488).

Q. 23 *Was Mary kept from having Original Sin?*
Yes, Mary was kept from having Original Sin (CCC 491).

We Pray:

HAIL MARY

Hail Mary, full of grace! The Lord is with thee.
Blessed art thou among women, and blessed is
the fruit of your womb, Jesus.
Holy Mary, Mother of God, pray for us sinners,
now and at the hour of our death. *Amen.*

GLORY BE

Glory be to the Father, and to the Son, and to the
Holy Spirit, as it was in the beginning, is now,
and ever shall be, world without end. *Amen.*

10   The Savior Is Born

"...you will find a baby wrapped in
swaddling cloths and lying in a manger."
Luke 2:12

One day, Mary and Joseph had to travel to **Bethlehem**. They looked and looked for a place to stay, but every inn was full and no one took them in. So they had to stay in a stable, a place where animals are kept.

This is where Jesus was born. Since Mary had no cradle for Him, she laid Him in a **manger**. A manger is a wooden box used to hold food for animals. The Son of God, our Savior, came here to earth as a poor, tiny, helpless baby.

Angels from Heaven appeared in the sky. They sang, "Glory to God in the highest. Peace on earth to men of good will."

Some **shepherds**—men who take care of sheep —saw the angels. The shepherds were afraid. "Do not be afraid," said the angels. "We have good news for you and for all people. Today in Bethlehem a Savior has been born! You will find Him lying in a manger." Then the angels left.

The shepherds were amazed. They said, "Let us go to Bethlehem and see this Child about whom the angels have spoken."

The shepherds hurried away and found Jesus, Mary, and Joseph. They knelt down to **worship** their Savior. To worship means to give your best love and praise to God. The shepherds remembered to thank God the Father for sending us His Son.

Christmas is the birthday of Jesus. This is an important day because if Jesus had not come, we could not go to Heaven, ever. There would be no Christmas trees, no presents, no Christmas lights, and no Christmas songs—nothing to make you happy. But Jesus did come and we have a wonderful time every year when we celebrate His birthday.

Words to Know:

Bethlehem   manger   shepherds   worship

Christmas

Q. 24 *Where was Jesus Christ born?*
Jesus Christ was born in a stable in
Bethlehem, and was placed in a manger
(CCC 525; Lk 2:7).

Q. 25 *Who is Jesus Christ?*
Jesus Christ is the Second Person of the
Blessed Trinity, the Son of God made man
(CCC 454, 495).

Q. 26 *Why did the Son of God become man?*
The Son of God became man to save us
from sin and to regain Heaven for us
(CCC 457–60).

We Pray:

Thank You, dear Jesus, for coming down
from Heaven to save us. Thank You for
Christmas time. Help us to get ready for
Your coming this year. *Amen.*

11 Three Wise Men Arrive

"Where is he who has been born king of the Jews?
For we have seen his star in the East,
and have come to worship him."

Matthew 2:2

Jesus came to save everybody. He loves the people of every part of the world and He loves them very, very much.

Three **wise men** came to Bethlehem from a far away land when Jesus was born. The wise men knew many things about God and the world He made by studying His creation. They did not get lost because they followed a star that brought them to Jesus. The wise men knew that Jesus was a great **king**. A king is someone who rules over a land. Jesus rules over all kings of the world and over the Kingdom of Heaven too. He is the King of Kings. So the wise men knelt before Jesus and gave Him gifts fit for a king. His Kingdom will never end!

Jesus was glad to see the wise men. Although He was a baby, He really was their God and King.

Can you do what the wise men did? Can you visit Jesus and give Him gifts? Yes, you can! Jesus is always waiting for you in church. You can visit Him any time the church is open.

If you are at home you can visit Jesus, too. All you have to do is stop what you are doing and talk to Him. God is everywhere and can always hear you.

Your gift to Jesus is your love for Him. Your prayers are a gift to Him. Your good deeds are a gift to Him too. Each time you chose right over wrong, that is a gift to Jesus.

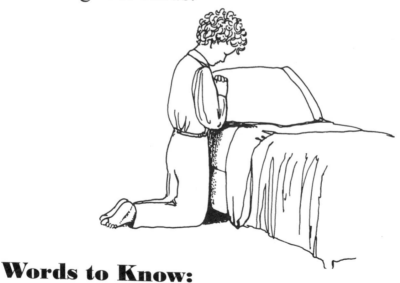

Words to Know:

wise men   king

Q. 27 *What did the wise men do when they found Jesus?*
They knelt before Jesus and gave Him gifts (CCC 528).

Q. 28 *Where can we go to kneel before Jesus?*
We can kneel before Jesus in the Blessed Sacrament (CCC 1373, 1378).

MORNING OFFERING

Dear Jesus, I give You my day and everything in it. Please keep me close to You, Your Mother Mary, and my guardian angel as I live today for Your glory. *Amen.*

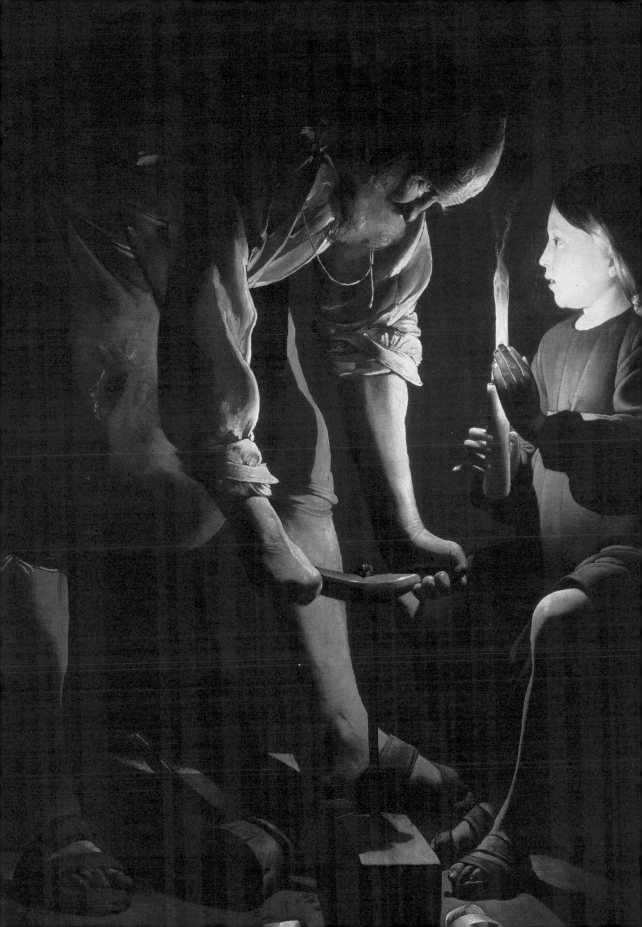

12   Jesus Grows Up

"And Jesus increased in wisdom and
in stature, and in favor with God and man."

Luke 2:52

The boy Jesus lived and worked and played in a little house in Nazareth. Jesus is the Son of God. Mary is His Mother. And Saint Joseph is His foster-father.

Saint Joseph did everything for Jesus just like a real father should. Saint Joseph was a **carpenter** who made chairs, tables, and many other things out of wood. Jesus liked to help him in the shop because He wanted to learn to be a carpenter, like Joseph.

Jesus loved His parents. He obeyed them and helped them with their work. He grew up and was strong and good. Jesus did all these things to show us how to **honor** our parents. When we love and obey them, we honor our parents and make our heavenly Father happy with us.

Words to Know:

carpenter   honor

Q. 29 *Is Saint Joseph the father of Jesus?*
No, Saint Joseph is the foster-father of
Jesus and the husband of Mary (CCC 484,
497).

Q. 30 *What does Jesus teach us in His family life?*
Jesus teaches us in His family life to love
and obey our parents (CCC 520, 532).

Litany to Saint Joseph

Let Us Pray:

Saint Joseph...
Foster-father of the Son of God...
Head of the Holy Family...
Joseph most just...
Joseph most strong...
Joseph most obedient...
Joseph most faithful...
Pillar of families...
Protector of Holy Church...

Pray for us.

52

13   Jesus Begins His Work

"And when Jesus had finished instructing his twelve disciples, he went on from there to teach and preach in their cities."

Matthew 11:1

When Jesus had grown up and was thirty years old, He left Nazareth. He knew it was time to begin His work. He walked from town to town and taught. He was a **teacher**, someone who shares with others the things that he knows so that they can know them too. He wanted everyone to learn about God.

He told people things about God that they never knew before, and He taught them how to love God better. Sometimes Jesus would teach large crowds, lots and lots of people. Sometimes He spoke to people one at a time.

Jesus liked to spend time with children. He liked to tell them how much their heavenly Father loved them. He put His arms around the children and then gave them His blessing.

Jesus picked twelve men to help him in a special way. These men were called the Twelve Apostles. They left their homes and went everywhere with Jesus. The Twelve Apostles listened to His teachings and then they told other people about Jesus. Later, additional men were chosen to be Apostles. The Apostles were the first bishops of the Church. They helped other people to follow Jesus. These other followers of Jesus we call disciples.

We, too, can be disciples of Jesus. We must listen to what our parents and teachers say about Him. We should tell others about Him. We should remember that Jesus is always near us.

Words to Know:

teacher   Apostles

Q. 31 *Who are the Apostles?*
The Apostles were special men who helped Jesus teach and lead his followers. Their successors today are called bishops (CCC 551).

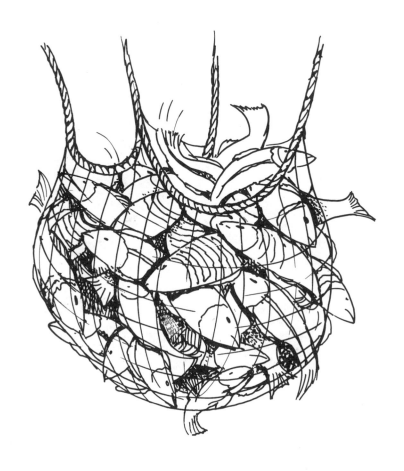

"Follow me and I will make you become fishers of men."

Mark 1:17

56

14 Jesus Tells the Good News

"Let the children come to me, and do not hinder them;
for to such belongs the kingdom of heaven."
Matthew 19:14

Jesus and His Apostles went from town to town. Jesus taught the people. He told everyone about the Good News of God's Kingdom everywhere He went.

The **Good News** is that God loves us all. Jesus told the people that God is their Father Who loves them very much. He told them that God wants them to be His children. He also said that God wants them to live in the Kingdom of Heaven.

Many people were happy to hear this Good News. They had waited all their lives for Jesus to come and show them the way to Heaven. Jesus taught them many other things. He taught them how to pray. He taught them how to love God and one another. Jesus came to show all of us the way to Heaven.

We can hear the Good News of Jesus too. The friends of Jesus wrote down the things He said and did while He was living here on earth. You can read about them in the **Bible**.

The Bible has other things in it, too. As you know, it tells the story of the sin of Adam and Eve. It tells of Noah, Abraham, and Moses. It also has prayers and songs. The Bible is God's book.

Words to Know:

Good News   Bible

> **Q. 32** *What did Jesus tell the people?*
> Jesus told the people the Good News of
> God's love for them (CCC 543–544).

15 Jesus Does Wonderful Things

"Truly you are the Son of God."
Matthew 14:33

To show us that He is really the Son of God, Jesus did many wonderful things that were beyond human power. We call these things **miracles**. Here are some of the miracles of Jesus:

One time, Jesus finished teaching five thousand people. Then it was late and everyone was hungry, but there wasn't enough food for everyone. So Jesus took five loaves of bread and two fishes and made them into enough for all of them, all five thousand people.

Another day Jesus and the Apostles were out on a boat when a big storm came. The Apostles were afraid the boat would sink so they called to Jesus, "Save us, Lord." Jesus told the wind and waves to be quiet, and everything grew calm, just like that! Only God can make the weather obey.

Another time a man came to Jesus. "Please come to my house," he said. "My little girl is sick." Jesus was sad about this so He went with him. On the way, someone from the man's house met them and he said, "It is too late. She's dead." But Jesus went right on to the house and He took the child's hand. "Get up little girl," Jesus said. The little girl opened her eyes and got up. Jesus had brought her back to life.

Jesus did many other miracles too. He made blind people see, He made deaf people hear, and He made sick people well.

Because Jesus is God, He could help anyone who asked Him for help. But He would only help them if it really was good for them, and if it was for the best. Jesus wants you to ask Him for help when you need it too. In the prayer Jesus gave us, we say, "Give us this day our daily bread," and that means asking for just about anything we need.

One day, some people carried a very sick man to Jesus. The man couldn't walk or even move his arms. But before Jesus made him better, He said, "Your sins are forgiven." Then He said, "Get up and walk." The man got up and walked. He felt so much better because his sins were gone too.

Because Jesus is God, He could heal the sick. Because Jesus is God, He can **forgive** sins. If we are sorry for our sins, Jesus will forgive them too.

Words to Know:

miracle   forgive

Q. 33 *Why did Jesus perform miracles?*
Jesus performed miracles to show us that He is truly the Son of God (CCC 515).

64

16   We Believe in Jesus

"And whatever you ask in prayer,
you will receive, if you have faith."
Matthew 21:22

Jesus is God's Son and the Savior of the world. He wants everyone to **believe** in Him. To believe is to accept that what someone says is true, even if you have never heard it before. That is why Jesus did all those miracles, and that is why He taught people. If you believe in Jesus, He will give you a reward, like in this real story:

Once there was a blind man. When Jesus was walking by, the blind man called out, "Jesus help me." "What do you want me to do?" Jesus asked. "Please make me see," begged the blind man. "Because you believe that I can do this, you will see," Jesus said. And He cured the blind man then and there.

Another day, a man came to ask Jesus to cure his dying servant, who was at home. "Lord," the man said, "I am not worthy (that means 'not good enough') for you to enter my house. But I know that if you just say one word, you can cure my servant from here." Jesus was so pleased with the man's faith that when the man came home, the servant was better. Jesus had cured him.

Jesus wants you to believe in Him too. You can pray:

Lord, I believe in You. Please help those who do not believe in You. *Amen.*

They did this:	And this is what happened:
The blind man believed in Jesus.	Jesus made him see.
The man with the dying servant believed in Jesus.	Jesus cured the servant.

You do this:	And this is what will happen:
You believe in Jesus.	Jesus promises to bring you to Heaven to be happy with Him forever.

Word to Know:

believe

Q. 34 *What is the reward for faith?*
The reward for faith is pleasing God and
attaining Heaven (CCC 161).

17   The Best Gift of All

"I made known to them your name, and I will make
it known, that the love with which you have
loved me may be in them, and I in them."

John 17:26

Jesus worked many miracles on earth. He taught us that He is God, and how much God loves us. But, Jesus knew that He was going to die soon. He loved us so very much that He found a way to be with us after He died.

The special supper Jesus shared with His Apostles on the night before He died is called the **Last Supper**. At the Last Supper, Jesus took bread and blessed it. He said, "Take this and eat of it. *This is My Body*." Then Jesus took a cup of wine and said, "*This is the chalice of My Blood*." Jesus changed bread and wine into His own Body and Blood. When the Apostles ate this Bread, Jesus lived inside them.

Then Jesus did something amazing. He gave His Apostles the power to change bread and wine into His

Body and Blood. The Apostles, in turn, passed on this power to all the bishops and priests who came after them, right up to today.

The **priest** at your church has received this power too. Because he has this power, when your priest offers **Mass**, he does what Jesus did at the Last Supper. When he says the words of Jesus, the bread and wine become the Body and Blood of Jesus. And when the people receive **Holy Communion**, Jesus comes to live in them. This is the best gift Jesus could have given us. It is the gift of Himself.

Words to Know:

Last Supper   Mass   priest

Holy Communion

Q. 35 *At the Last Supper, what did Jesus do with the bread and wine?*
At the Last Supper, Jesus changed the bread and wine into His Body and Blood (CCC 1339).

Q. 36 *Why can priests today change bread and wine into the Body and Blood of Jesus?*
Jesus gave this power to His Apostles and they gave it to the bishops and priests who came after them (CCC 1341).

Q. 37 *Why is Holy Communion a special gift from God?*
Holy Communion is a special gift from God because, in Communion, Jesus Himself comes to live in us (CCC 1384).

Jesus said to them, "I am the bread of life; he who comes to me shall not hunger, and he who believes in me shall never thirst.... I am the living bread which came down from heaven; if any one eats of this bread, he will live for ever; and the bread which I shall give for the life of the world is my flesh."

John 6:35, 51

71

18　　Jesus Dies for Us

"Greater love has no man than this,
that a man lay down his life for his friends."
John 15:13

The Last Supper happened on a Thursday. That
night, after the Supper was over, Jesus went out to
a garden to pray. He knew that soon He would be
killed, but He wanted to give His life to save us.
When soldiers came and took Jesus away the Apostles
were afraid, but Jesus was brave. The next day, on
Friday, they beat Him with whips. They pressed a
crown of thorns onto His head and made fun of Him.

Because Jesus was God He could have stopped
them from hurting Him, but He did not. That is
because He wanted to suffer for us, because He loves
us. His suffering and dying would bring us the gift of
grace, God's life, and the ability to go to Heaven.

Later that day, bad men decided to kill Jesus.
Jesus had to carry a heavy Cross through the city of
Jerusalem and sometimes it made Him fall.

Mary met her Son on the way and she suffered very much when she saw the way people were hurting Jesus. Then a man named Simon helped Jesus to carry the Cross until they came to the top of a hill. That is when soldiers crucified Jesus (this means they nailed Him to a wooden cross to die). Mary and Saint John the Apostle stood by Jesus the whole time because they loved Him so much.

After three hours, Jesus died. His friends took Him down from the Cross and buried Him.

Jesus died to make up for Adam's sin and for our sins too. Jesus died to win back the gift of grace for us. Jesus died so that we could live in Heaven forever and ever. We call the day He died **Good Friday** because it is good that Jesus died and opened up the gates of Heaven.

Words to Know:

Good Friday

Q. 38 *How did Jesus suffer?*
Jesus was scourged, crowned with thorns, He carried His Cross, He was crucified, and He died (CCC 572, 596, 619).

Q. 39 *Why did Jesus suffer?*
Jesus suffered to atone for Adam's sin and our sins, and to open again the gates of Heaven (CCC 615).

We Pray:

Thank you, Jesus, for loving me so much.
I am sorry my sins made You suffer.
Thank You for giving Your life for me. *Amen.*

76

19   Jesus Was Raised to New Life

"He is not here; for he has risen, as he said.
Come, see the place where he lay."

Matthew 28:6

On the third day after Jesus died, something wonderful happened. Jesus rose from the dead, which means that He came back to life! That day was the very first **Easter Sunday**. We call this great miracle the **Resurrection**.

Mary and the Apostles were so happy to see Jesus alive again. And we are glad that our Savior is alive too. Because Jesus rose from the dead, we too can share in His life and live forever!

At Mass on Easter Sunday we sing joyful songs that praise and thank God:

"The Lord is Risen!"
"**Alleluia!** Alleluia! Alleluia!"

Jesus won the gift of grace for us so now we, too, can come back to life after we die. We will go to Heaven to be with Jesus. One day, our bodies will also rise from the dead and be with us in Heaven too. Because Jesus rose from the dead with His body, we know we will be able to live with Jesus in Heaven— body and soul.

Words to Know:

Easter   Alleluia   Resurrection

Q. 40 *After His death, what did Jesus do?*
After His death, Jesus rose again from the dead, taking up His body that had been buried (CCC 646).

Q. 41 *How long did the body of Jesus remain buried?*
The body of Jesus remained buried from Friday evening to the day that we now call Easter Sunday (CCC 639).

20   Jesus Begins the Church

"And I tell you, you are Peter, and on this rock
I will build my Church, and the gates of Hades
shall not prevail against it."
Matthew 16:18

Jesus was alive and with His Apostles again. But He was going to go up to Heaven. Jesus wanted all people to know the Good News of God's love. He wanted people to know Him and He wanted His work to continue on earth. To continue His work, He started His **Church**.

People who belong to the Church can learn about Jesus and receive the gift of grace. He continues to work in and through the Church, so we can come to know His love for us.

Jesus made His Apostles the leaders of His Church and they were the first **bishops**. Then He named **Peter** the head of the Apostles and the very first **Pope**. Do you know who your Pope and bishop are?

Words to Know:

Church   Pope   bishop   Peter

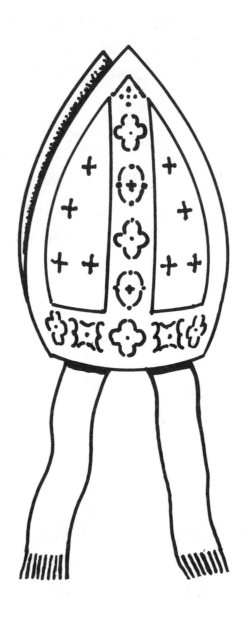

Q. 42 *What is the Church?*
The Church is the group of baptized persons who profess the Catholic Faith and come together to worship God. (CCC 751–52).

Q. 43 *By whom was the Church founded?*
The Church was founded by Jesus Christ (CCC 763–66).

Q. 44 *Who is the Pope?*
The Pope is the successor of Saint Peter. He is the visible head of the Catholic Church (CCC 882).

21 Jesus Goes Back to Heaven

"...as they were looking on, he was lifted up,
and a cloud took him out of their sight."

Acts 1:9

Jesus spent forty days with His Apostles after He rose from the dead. He told them many things that they should know. Then it was time for Him to go back to God, His Father.

So He took the Apostles to the top of a mountain. "Go," He said. "Teach everyone and baptize them in the Name of the Father and of the Son and of the Holy Spirit." Jesus promised to be with them always even if they could not see Him. He promised to send the **Holy Spirit** to help them, too. Then Jesus rose up to Heaven. We call this the **Ascension**.

The Apostles watched and watched until they could not see Jesus anymore. Then two angels came. They said, "Someday Jesus will come again." Jesus will come again at the end of the world.

Words to Know:

Ascension   Holy Spirit

Q. 45 *What did Jesus do after His Resurrection?*
After His Resurrection, Jesus remained
on earth for forty days, then He ascended
to Heaven (CCC 659).

22   The Holy Spirit Comes

"And they were all filled with the Holy Spirit..."
Acts 2:4

For nine days, the Apostles waited for the Holy Spirit to come to them. They stayed in a house with Mary and prayed and prayed. On the tenth day something wonderful happened. The Apostles heard the sound of a great wind. And then the Holy Spirit came! This day is called **Pentecost**.

The Holy Spirit filled their souls with grace and He filled their hearts with love for God. He helped them to remember and to understand all the things Jesus had taught them. He made them very brave and strong so they could continue Jesus' work here on earth.

Now the Apostles could go out and tell all the world about Jesus, just as He asked them to do. So the Apostles went out. Peter began to teach the Good News. "Believe in Jesus, be **baptized**, and you will be saved," Peter said.

Many people believed Peter's words, and about three thousand were baptized that very day. Already the Church was beginning to grow.

The Holy Spirit is alive in the Church today. He helps the Pope and the bishops to teach the truth about God. He helps us to love one another and become holy.

Words to Know:

baptized   Pentecost

Q. 46 *What happened on Pentecost?*
On Pentecost, the Holy Spirit came to Mary and the Apostles (CCC 731; Acts 2:1–4).

Q. 47 *What did the Holy Spirit do for the Apostles?*
The Holy Spirit gave grace to the Apostles, and the courage to continue Jesus' work (CCC 737, 739).

SECVND ESV
VM·MA CHR
·TH·
LIBER IST·
FILII D
GENERA AVID·
TIONIS·

INITIV
NDV EVANGE
MMAR LII IESV
CVM· CHRIST

SECVN
DVM
LVCAM
FVIT
IN·DIE

SEC IN·PRIN
BV VN CIPIO ER
HERO AT VERB
DIS·RE OAVM·ET·V
GIS· NNERBVM F

23 The Blessed Trinity

"Go therefore and make disciples of all nations,
baptizing them in the name of the Father
and of the Son and of the Holy Spirit."

Matthew 28:19

There is only one God. There are three Divine Persons in one God: God the Father, God the Son, and God the Holy Spirit. The Father is God. The Son is God. The Holy Spirit is God. But together They are one God.

We call the three Persons in one God the **Blessed Trinity**. **God the Father** is the First Person of the Blessed Trinity. **God the Son** is the Second Person of the Blessed Trinity. He became the man Whom we call Jesus and Who died to save us from sin. **God the Holy Spirit** is the Third Person of the Blessed Trinity. He helps us to pray and to love one another.

The three Persons of the Blessed Trinity had no beginning. They always were and always will be.

The three Persons are equal. The Father is not greater than the Son. The Son is not greater than the Holy Spirit.

We know there are three Persons in one God because Jesus told us about it. But we cannot really understand how God can be both three and one. That is called a **mystery** and we will have to wait until Heaven to understand it better. But it can help if you think about a family. In a family there are the mother, father, and children, all different persons, but they are one family. In the Blessed Trinity there are three Persons, but one God.

We often begin our prayers by calling on the Blessed Trinity. We say, "In the Name of the Father and of the Son and of the Holy Spirit." When we say these words, we make the Sign of the Cross on our bodies. And it reminds us that Jesus saved us by dying on a Cross.

When my soul is filled with grace, the Blessed Trinity lives in me!

Words to Know:

Blessed Trinity   God the Father   God the Son

God the Holy Spirit   mystery

Q. 48 *Who is the First Person of the Blessed Trinity?*
The First Person of the Blessed Trinity is God the Father (CCC 254).

Q. 49 *Who is the Second Person of the Blessed Trinity?*
The Second Person of the Blessed Trinity is God the Son (CCC 254).

Q. 50 *Who is the Third Person of the Blessed Trinity?*
The Third Person of the Blessed Trinity is God the Holy Spirit (CCC 254).

Q. 51 *Has God always existed?*
God has always been and always will be (CCC 202).

We Pray:

GLORY BE

Glory be to the Father, and to the Son, and to the Holy Spirit, as it was in the beginning is now, and ever shall be, world without end. *Amen.*

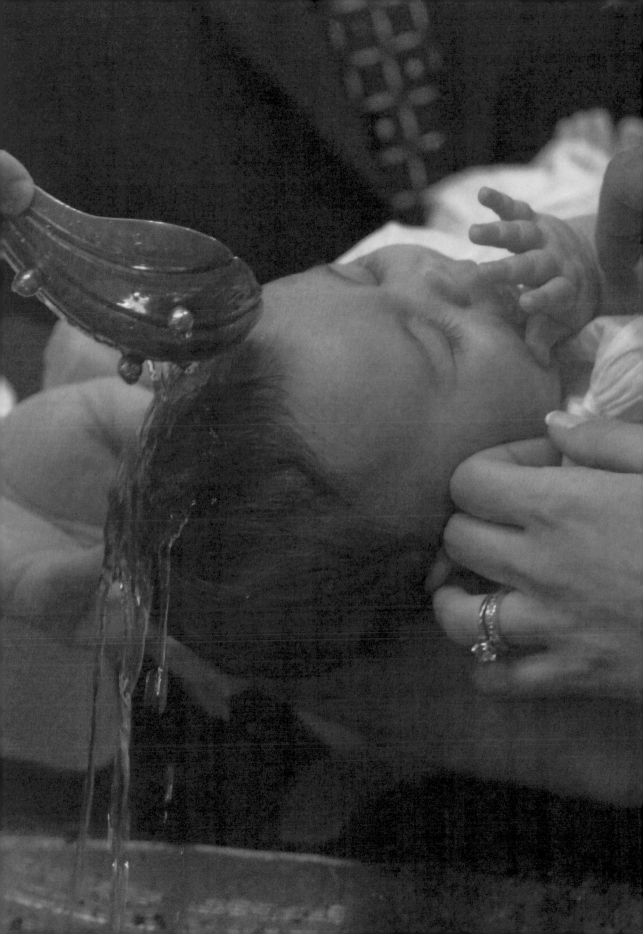

24   God Gives You His Life

"We were buried therefore with him by baptism into death,
so that as Christ was raised from the dead by the glory
of the Father, we too might walk in newness of life."

Romans 6:4

When Adam and Eve sinned, it meant that all the
people born after him would have Adam's sin. It is
called Original Sin because it was the first sin. You
were born with Original Sin on your soul. This means
that when you were born, there was none of God's life
of grace in your soul. You were made for Baptism.

The Sacrament of Baptism washes away the guilt
of Original Sin. When you are baptized, your soul is
filled with the grace that Jesus won for you. It gives
you God's life. That way you can reach Heaven.

Baptism makes you a child of God. And Baptism
makes you a member of God's family, which is the
Church.

Jesus wants all of us to share in His life and
become children of God. Jesus said to His Apostles,

"Go and baptize all people." Like the Apostles, the priest is Jesus' helper. That is why the priest baptizes people.

When the priest baptizes a baby, he pours water on the baby's head and says, "I baptize you in the Name of the Father and of the Son and of the Holy Spirit." Now the baby is a child of God. Now the baby's soul is holy and pleasing to God.

Not everyone is baptized as a baby, but most people are. Ask your parents about your own Baptism. They can tell you all about when you were baptized. Maybe they even took a picture of your Baptism.

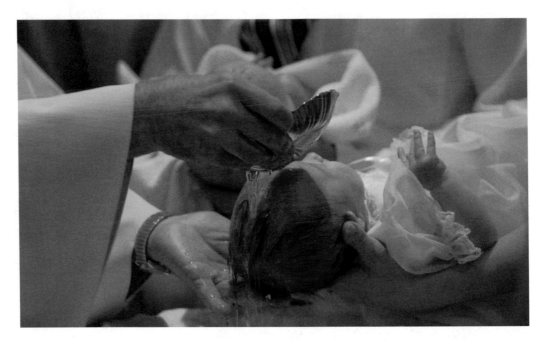

Words to Know:

Sacrament   Baptism

Q. 52 *How is Original Sin taken away?*
Original Sin is taken away by the
Sacrament of Baptism (CCC 1263).

Q. 53 *What is Baptism?*
Baptism is the Sacrament that makes us
followers of Christ, sons of God, and
members of His Church (CCC 1213).

Q. 54 *What is a Sacrament?*
A Sacrament is an outward sign made by
Christ to give grace (CCC 774, 1131).

---

*"For just as the body is one and has many
members, and all the members of the body,
though many, are one body, so it is with Christ.
For by one Spirit we were all baptized into one
body..."*

1 Corinthians 12:12–13

25   Many Gifts from God

"Man shall not live by bread alone, but by every word
that proceeds from the mouth of God."

Matthew 4:4

God has given you many gifts. He made you.
He gave you a wonderful world in which to live. He
gave you your family. God also sent His Son to be
your Savior. And He gave you the gift of His life,
called grace, in the Sacrament of Baptism.

Do you wonder how you can thank God for all
He has given you? One of the best things you can do
is to sit quietly at Mass and listen to and join in the
prayers.

At every Mass we hear God's Word; God is
speaking to us. We listen to a special message from
God's book, which is called the Holy Bible. And we
hear the Good News about Jesus from a part of the
Bible called the **Gospel**.

Jesus is with us at Mass. He offers Himself to

God the Father at every Mass, just as He did on Good Friday. We can offer ourselves with Jesus, too.

At every Mass we should remember the Last Supper that Jesus had with the Apostles and how He changed the bread and wine into His Body and Blood. God has given priests the power to do what Jesus did. That is why the priest takes bread in his hands and says the words of Jesus:

"This is my Body"

and the bread becomes the Body of Jesus. Then the priest takes the cup of wine and says:

"This is the chalice of my Blood"

and the wine becomes the Blood of Jesus.

We do not see Jesus on the altar, but He is really there. Jesus is God and He can do anything.

Someday, you will be able to receive Jesus in Holy Communion. Then you will be closer to Him than ever before.

Word to Know:

Gospel

Q. 55 *What happens during Mass?*
During the Mass, Jesus comes to earth in the Eucharist. We remember the Last Supper, His sacrifice, and His death on the Cross (CCC 1365–67).

Q. 56 *Why has Christ given Himself to us in the Holy Eucharist?*
Christ has given Himself to us in the Holy Eucharist to be the life and food of our souls (CCC 1384).

We Pray:

Jesus, please come to me soon. I want so much to receive You. *Amen.*

"Truly, truly, I say to you, unless you eat the flesh of the Son of man and drink his blood, you have no life in you; he who eats my flesh and drinks my blood has eternal life, and I will raise him up at the last day...."

John 6:53–54

26   Our Mother, Mary

"Then he said to the disciple,
'Behold, your mother!'"

John 19:27

Before Jesus went back to His heavenly Father, He left us a special gift. He gave us His Mother for our very own! From her place in Heaven she watches over you with so much love.

You can ask your Blessed Mother to pray for you when you need help. She will pray to God for you. She will help you to get to Heaven.

Jesus is the King of Heaven. Mary is the **Queen of Heaven**. Mary is the Queen of all the angels and all the saints.

Mary is the special friend of children. She has asked all boys and girls to pray and make **sacrifices** so that there will be peace in the world. A sacrifice is when a person goes without something, out of love for God.

Words to Know:

Queen of Heaven   sacrifice

> **Q. 57** *Who is Mary?*
> Mary is the Mother of Jesus and the
> Queen of Heaven, earth, angels, and
> men (CCC 501, 963, 966).

We Pray:

HAIL MARY

Hail Mary, full of Grace! The Lord is with thee.
Blessed art thou among women, and blessed
is the fruit of thy womb, Jesus.
Holy Mary, Mother of God, pray for us sinners,
now and at the hour of our death. *Amen.*

Litany to Mary

Let Us Pray:

Holy Mary...
Holy Mother of God...
Mother of divine grace...
Mother of our Savior...
Health of the sick...
Help of Christians...
Queen of angels...
Queen of prophets...
Queen of Apostles...
Queen of all saints...
Queen of peace...

Pray for us.

27   Following Jesus

"No greater joy can I have than this,
to hear that my children follow the truth."
3 John 1:4

When we play "Follow the Leader," we walk behind someone else and we do whatever the person in front of us does. The "leader" doesn't take us to any place special because it is only a game.

But Jesus is our leader on the road of life and that is not a game. It is real. By following Him, we can come to the Kingdom of Heaven. By doing whatever Jesus does, we learn how to live as God's children.

These are some of the things Jesus did that we should follow. Jesus always obeyed His Mother and foster-father, Saint Joseph. He told them the truth. He did the work they asked Him to do. He was kind to everyone. He shared with others. He forgave those who hurt Him. You can do these things too.

Jesus also showed us how to pray. To pray means to talk with God. You can say the prayers you have learned or you can tell God what you are thinking about. God is interested in anything you have to say and anything you think, or even feel.

Every morning when you wake up, you should kneel down and make the Sign of the Cross. You should offer God everything you will do and say and think that day. At night, kneel down beside your bed and thank God for the things He gave you during the day.

You can ask Him to bless all the people you love and all the people everywhere. Try to remember if you did anything wrong that day, and then tell God you are sorry. Ask Him to make you a better boy or girl tomorrow.

Remember, you can pray anytime or anywhere, and about anything. You can ask God to help people who are sick or unhappy. You can ask God to make you a **saint**. A saint is a good person who has died and gone to Heaven to be with God.

Jesus taught us to love God with all our hearts. You can show God that you love Him, too. One way is to work hard to learn about Him. You can try to be good even when it is very difficult. And you can go to Mass and learn to say the prayers of the Mass. With Jesus, you can offer yourself to the Father at Mass.

God has given you so many gifts. Your gift to God is to live as His good child, to thank Him and to love Him.

Word to Know:

saint

Q. 58 *What is prayer?*
Prayer is talking to God (CCC 2559).

28   Jesus Will Come Again

"And when I go and prepare a place for you,
I will come again and will take you to myself,
that where I am you may be also."

John 14:3

Do you know why you are here on earth? You are here to learn to know God, to love, and to **serve** God. If you learn how to do these things, you will be ready to live with God forever and ever in Heaven.

We are on earth for only a short time, but Heaven never ends. Heaven is our true home, the place where we will always be happy with Jesus, with Mary, and with those we love.

Someday, the world will end. Then Jesus will come again. He will take all the good people to Heaven with Him. The souls of all the people who have died will be united with their bodies again.

Do you want to start on the road to Heaven? All

you have to do is try your best to love God every day. Ready! Set! Go!

Word to Know:

serve

> **Q. 59** *Why did God make you?*
> God made you to know, love, and serve Him in this world, and to be happy with Him forever in Heaven (CCC 260, 358).

We Go to Mass

"And beginning with Moses and all the prophets,
he interpreted to them in all the Scriptures the things
concerning himself....When he was at table with them, he
took the bread and blessed and broke it,
and gave it to them. And their eyes were opened
and they recognized him."
Luke 24:27, 30–31

One of God's Laws says, "You must keep the Lord's Day holy." Sunday is the Lord's Day because Jesus rose from the dead on a Sunday. This is why every Sunday we go to Church to **worship** God at Mass.

When we come into Church, we use Holy Water to make the Sign of the Cross. This reminds us of our Baptism and that we are God's children. Before we take our seats, we **genuflect** (kneel down on our right knee) and make the Sign of the Cross to honor Jesus in the tabernacle. Before Mass begins, we kneel down and talk to God for a while.

The priest comes in while we sing a hymn. He begins Mass with the Sign of the Cross: "In the Name of the Father and of the Son and of the Holy Spirit. *Amen.*"

Then the priest asks us to think about how we have disobeyed God. And we think, "Dear Jesus, I am sorry for my sins. I want to love You more and more."

And then we usually say: "Glory to God in the highest!" We use the same words the angels sang at Bethlehem to praise God for his goodness.

After that we sit down and hear two readings and a Psalm from the Bible. We should listen carefully and try to understand God's message to us.

Then we stand and listen while the priest reads from the Gospel. The Gospel is the part of the Bible that tells us what Jesus said and did. Through the words of the Gospel, Jesus teaches us about our heavenly Father. Then the priest talks to us to help us understand God's Word.

After that we stand and say the **Creed**. The Creed is what we believe about God and His Church.

Now it is time for the Offertory. That is when we offer gifts of bread and wine, and we offer our money to help take care of our church. We offer ourselves with Jesus to God the Father.

At the Last Supper, Jesus changed bread and wine into His own Body and Blood. At Mass, the priest takes the place of Jesus. He takes a special round piece of bread and says the words of Jesus:

"This is my Body."

Then it is not bread anymore. It is the real Body of Jesus.

Next the priest takes the cup filled with wine and says:

"This is the chalice of my Blood."

Now it is the Blood of Jesus. We worship Jesus when the priest holds Him up and we tell Him how happy we are that He is with us.

Then we stand and say the prayer Jesus gave us, the Our Father. We may give the Sign of Peace to each other to show that we want to love one another, just as Jesus taught us.

The people go up to receive Jesus in Holy Communion. Someday you will make your First Communion.

After a last prayer, the priest says, "Go forth, the Mass is ended." And we answer, "Thanks be to God."

After the priest leaves, we should kneel down to thank Jesus and say goodbye to Him.

Thank You, Jesus, for the gift of the Mass.
Help me to love God and others this week. *Amen.*

Words to Know:

worship   genuflect   Creed

Words to Know

The numbers in parentheses correspond to the chapter in which each word can be found.

Abraham (7): A man who lived before Jesus was born. He always did what God wanted, even when it was difficult. He is known as the father of the Jewish people, and our father in faith.

Adam (5): The first man that God made. Eve was the first woman that God made. Adam and Eve are our first parents because everyone came from them.

Alleluia (19): A word that means, "Praise God." We say this at Eastertime to show how happy we are that Jesus rose from the dead.

angels (3): Invisible spirits created by God. Angels are God's helpers.

Apostles (13): Apostles are people sent out by another to help do his work. Jesus had twelve Apostles whom He sent out to tell others about Him after He went back to Heaven. They became the first bishops.

ark (7): A large boat. God told Noah to build an ark to save himself, his family, and the animals from the great flood.

Ascension (21): The return of Jesus to Heaven forty days after Easter.

Baptism (24): Baptism is a Sacrament that takes

away Original Sin and gives us grace. It also makes us followers of Christ, sons of God, and members of His Church.

baptized (22): To receive the Sacrament of Baptism.

believe (16): To believe is to accept that what someone says is true, even if you have never heard it before. We believe that Jesus is telling us the truth about Himself and His Father because as God He cannot lie.

Bethlehem (10): The town where Jesus was born.

Bible (14): The holy book that God gave us. It tells us about God's special people and about the beginning of the Church.

bishop (20): A man who has received the power from the Apostles to carry on their work. He takes care of a large group of Catholics.

body (4): The part of you that you can see. The other part of you is your soul.

carpenter (12): Someone who makes chairs, tables, and many other things out of wood. Saint Joseph, the foster-father of Jesus, was a carpenter.

Christmas (10): The day we celebrate Jesus' birth.

Church (20): This is the Catholic Church that Jesus founded. The followers of Jesus are part of the Church. They come together to worship God. The Pope and the bishops are the leaders of the Church.

create (3): To create is to make something out of nothing. God is our Creator. That means He made us and all things out of nothing.

Creed (We Go to Mass): What we believe about God and His Church.

devils (3): Angels who chose to become bad by turning away from God.

Easter Sunday (19): The Sunday that Jesus rose from the dead.

Eve (5): The first woman that God made. Adam was the first man that God made. Adam and Eve are called our first parents because everyone came from them.

faith (7): Faith is a gift from God that makes us able to believe all that God tells us.

forgive (15): To forgive is to pardon someone who has done something wrong. Only God can forgive sins.

Gabriel (9): The angel that God sent to Mary. He asked her if she would be Jesus' Mother.

genuflect (We Go to Mass): To kneel down on your right knee and then stand up again.

God the Father (23): God the Father is God, the First Person of the Blessed Trinity.

God the Holy Spirit (23): God the Holy Spirit is God, the Third Person of the Blessed Trinity.

God the Son (23): God the Son is God, the Second Person of the Blessed Trinity. God the Son became man and is the Divine Person of Jesus, our Savior.

Good Friday (18): The day that Jesus died on the Cross for our sins and opened the gates of Heaven.

Good News (14): The message that Jesus came to tell us: God loves us all and wants us to be with Him in the Kingdom of Heaven.

Gospel (25): A part of the Bible that tells the Good News of Jesus. In the Gospels, Jesus' friends wrote down many of the things He said and did while He was living here on earth.

grace (5): The life of God in our soul.

guardian angel (4): A special angel given to each person by God who helps to take care of him.

Heaven (2): Heaven is God's home and a place of perfect happiness. God wants us to come to be happy with Him forever in Heaven.

Holy Communion (17): The Body and Blood of Jesus that Catholics receive during Mass.

Holy Spirit (21): The Holy Spirit is God, the Third Person of the Blessed Trinity.

honor (12): To love and obey someone.

Jesus (9): Jesus is God, the Second Person of the Blessed Trinity made man.

Joseph (9): Joseph is the foster-father of Jesus and the husband of Mary.

king (11): Someone who rules over a land. Jesus is King not only of the whole world, but of the Kingdom of Heaven as well.

Last Supper (17): The holy supper that Jesus ate with His Apostles the night before He died. At the Last Supper Jesus gave us His Body and Blood, and He gave the Apostles the power to change bread and wine into His Body and Blood.

manger (10): A wooden box used to hold food for

animals. Mary had to use a manger for the baby Jesus when He was born.

Mary (9): The Mother of Jesus. Mary is our Mother too.

Mass (17): At Mass, Jesus offers Himself to the Father just as He did on Good Friday. Through the words of the priest, the bread and wine become the Body and Blood of Jesus, as they did at the Last Supper.

miracles (15): Wonderful things done by the power of God and that can only be done by God.

Moses (8): The first prophet. God gave Moses the Ten Commandments.

mystery (23): Something that we know because God has told us, but that we cannot understand completely. The Blessed Trinity is a mystery.

Nazareth (9): The town where Jesus lived with Mary and Joseph.

New Testament (14): The second part of the Bible starting with the life of Jesus Christ.

Noah (7): The good man who obeyed God and built an ark to save his family and the animals from the great flood.

obedient (7): To be obedient is to be someone who obeys; someone who does what he is told to do.

obey (6): To obey is to do what one is told to do. Everyone should obey God's Laws.

Old Testament (14): The first part of the Bible; it tells us about God preparing the people for the coming of Jesus.

Original Sin (6): The very first sin committed by Adam and Eve. Adam and Eve are our first parents so we are all born with Original Sin.

Our Father (1): The special prayer that Jesus gave us. We say it to our Father in Heaven.

Pentecost (22): The tenth day after the Ascension when the Holy Spirit came down upon Mary and the Apostles.

Peter (20): The very first Pope. Peter was a fisherman and one of the twelve Apostles chosen by Jesus.

Pope (20): The man who holds the place of Jesus as the visible head of the Catholic Church until He comes again at the end of the world.

prayer (1, 27): Talking with God. You can use prayers you have learned or just tell Him what you are thinking.

priest (17): A man who has received the power from Jesus to forgive sins and offer Mass.

promise (6): To promise is to say you are going to do something and really mean it. God promised to send us a Savior.

prophets (8): Holy men who prepared people for the coming of Jesus, the Savior.

Queen of Heaven (26): The name we give to our Mother Mary to show that she has the highest place in Heaven next to Jesus. She is above all the angels and other saints.

Resurrection (19): The raising of a body from the

dead. Jesus rose from the dead on Easter Sunday. Our bodies will be raised from the dead at the end of the world to be reunited with our souls.

Sacrament (24): A Sacrament is an outward sign instituted by God to confer grace. There are seven Sacraments.

sacrifice (26): A sacrifice is a way to show God how much we love Him by giving up something that we like.

saint (27): A holy person who loved God very much on earth and who is now in Heaven. God wants all of us to be saints.

Saint John the Baptist (8): The cousin of Jesus and the last prophet. He told people to be sorry for their sins. He also baptized them to help them prepare for the coming of the Savior.

Savior (6): The one God promised to send to save us from our sins and open the gates of Heaven. Jesus is the Savior.

serve (28): To serve is to follow orders or to help or do work for someone else. We serve God when we do what He wants us to do.

shepherds (10): Men who take care of sheep. When Jesus was born some shepherds were the first to hear the Good News.

Sign of the Cross (2): The shape of the cross that we make by touching our forehead, chest, and shoulders. This shows that we believe that Jesus died on the

Cross for us. We also show that we believe in the Blessed Trinity.

sin (6): Sin is saying no to God. It is any bad thing that we choose to do, think, or say. When we sin, we turn away from God.

soul (4): The soul is the part of us that thinks, loves, and chooses what to do. The soul is invisible. The soul never dies.

teacher (13): Someone who shares with others the things that he knows so that they can know them too.

Ten Commandments (8): The moral laws that God gave to Moses on Mount Sinai. These Laws tell us how to live as God wants us to live.

Trinity, Blessed (23): The three Divine Persons in one God. The Blessed Trinity is a mystery.

wise men (11): Men who knew many things about God and the world He made by studying His creation. Three wise men came to Jesus when He was a baby and brought Him presents fit for a king.

worship (10, We Go to Mass): To worship is to give your best love and praise to God.

The Alphabet

A is for **Apostles**, the twelve friends of Jesus.

A is also for **angels**, **Abraham**, **Adam**, **Alleluia**, **ark**, and **Ascension**.

B is for **Baptism**, the first Sacrament. **Baptism** washes away sins and makes us God's children.

B is also for **Bethlehem**, **Bible**, **bishop**, **body**, and **believe**.

C is for **Catholic Church**, God's family.

C is also for **Cross**, **Christmas**, **Creator**, **Creed**, and **carpenter**.

D is for **devil**, an angel who turned away from God and who wants us to sin.

E is for **Easter**, the day Jesus rose from the dead.

F is for **forgive**. Jesus washes away sin.

G is for **God, our Father**, Who made everything and loves us all.

G is also for **Gabriel**, **Good Friday**, **Good News**, **Gospel**, **grace**, **genuflect**, and **guardian angel**.

H is for **Heaven**, where we will be happy with God forever.

H is for **Holy Communion** and **Holy Spirit**.

I is for **Israel**, the land where Jesus was born.

J is for **Jesus**, the Son of God. He is our Savior and brother.

J is also for **John the Baptist** and **Joseph**.

K is for **king**. Jesus is the King of Heaven and earth.

L is for **Last Supper**, the dinner that Jesus ate with His Apostles the night before He died.

M is for **Mary**, the Mother of God and our Blessed Mother too.

M is also for **Mass**, **Moses**, **manger**, **miracle**, and **mystery**.

N is for **Noah**. He obeyed God and saved his family and the animals from the flood.

N is also for **Nazareth**.

O is for **obey**. We must obey God's Laws. God also wants us to obey our parents.

O is also for **Our Father** and **Original Sin**.

P is for **Pope**, the leader of the whole Church. He has the power to teach all Christians.

P is also for **prayer**, **Peter**, **priest**, **promise**, and **prophet**.

Q is for **quiet**. We are quiet in church so we can pray and hear God's Word.

Q is also for **Queen of Heaven**.

R is for **Resurrection**, the moment when Jesus was raised to new life.

S is for **saint**, someone who loved God on earth and is now in Heaven. There is a saint for almost every name. We all want to be saints too.

S is also for **Savior, sin, sacrifice, serve, shepherd, Sign of the Cross**, and **soul**.

T is for Blessed **Trinity,** three Persons in one God: The Father, Son, and Holy Spirit.

T is also for **Ten Commandments** and **teacher**.

U is for **unity**. All Catholics share the same faith in Jesus. We hope that everyone will share our faith someday.

V is for **victory**. Jesus won back the life of grace for us. He conquered sin and death.

W is for **wise men**. Three **wise men** came to adore the Child Jesus and bring Him presents.

W is also for **worship**.

X is **Xmas**, which is another name for Christmas. The X stands for Christ, a name for Jesus.

Y is for **you**, a member of God's family. You can know, love, and serve God. You can be a saint!

Z is for **zeal**, another name for our love of God.

WE PRAY

THE SIGN OF THE CROSS

In the Name of the Father, and of the Son,
and of the Holy Spirit. *Amen.*

OUR FATHER

Our Father, Who art in Heaven, hallowed be
Thy Name; Thy Kingdom come; Thy will be
done on earth as it is in Heaven. Give us this day
our daily bread, and forgive us our trespasses, as
we forgive those who trespass against us; and lead us
not into temptation, but deliver us from evil.
Amen.

PRAYER TO MY GUARDIAN ANGEL

Angel of God, my guardian dear,
To whom God's love commits me here,
Ever this day be at my side,
To light and guard, to rule and guide. *Amen.*

MORNING OFFERING

Dear Jesus, I give You my day and everything in it.
Please keep me close to You, Your Mother Mary,
and my guardian angel as I live today for Your glory.
Amen.

HAIL MARY

Hail Mary, full of grace! The Lord is with thee.
Blessed art thou among women, and blessed is the
fruit of thy womb, Jesus.
Holy Mary, Mother of God, pray for us sinners, now
and at the hour of our death. *Amen.*

GLORY BE

Glory Be to the Father, and to the Son, and to the
Holy Spirit, as it was in the beginning, is now, and
ever shall be, world without end. *Amen.*

ADDITIONAL CATHOLIC PRAYERS

SAINT MICHAEL PRAYER

Saint Michael the Archangel, defend us in battle.
Be our protection against the wickedness and
snares of the devil. May God rebuke him, we
humbly pray, and do thou, O prince of the
heavenly hosts, by the power of God, thrust into Hell
Satan and all the evil spirits, who prowl about the
world seeking the ruin of souls. *Amen.*

THE PRAYER OF FATIMA

O my Jesus, forgive us our sins, save us from the
fires of Hell, and lead all souls into Heaven,
especially those in most need of Thy mercy.
Amen.

SPIRITUAL COMMUNION

My Jesus, as I cannot receive Thee now in the
Most Holy Blessed Sacrament, I ask Thee to come
into my heart, and make it like Thy heart. *Amen.*

MORNING OFFERING

O Jesus, through the Immaculate Heart of Mary,
I offer You my prayers, works, joys, and sufferings
of this day, for the intentions of Your Sacred
Heart, in union with the Holy Sacrifice of the
Mass throughout the world, in reparation for my
sins, and for the conversion of all sinners. *Amen.*

ACT OF FAITH

O my God, I firmly believe that You are one
God in three Divine Persons: Father, Son, and
Holy Spirit. I believe that Your divine Son
became man and died for our sins, and that He
will come to judge the living and the dead. I
believe these and all the truths which the Holy
Catholic Church teaches, because You revealed
them, who can neither deceive nor be deceived.
Amen.

ACT OF HOPE

O my God, relying on Your infinite goodness
and promises, I hope to obtain pardon of my
sins, the help of Your grace, and life everlasting,
through the merits of Jesus Christ, my Lord and
Redeemer. *Amen.*

ACT OF LOVE

O my God, I love You above all things with my whole heart and soul, because You are all good and worthy of all my love. I love my neighbor as myself for love of You. I forgive all who have injured me, and I ask pardon for all whom I have injured. *Amen.*

ACT OF CONTRITION

O my God, I am heartily sorry for having offended You. I detest all my sins because of Your just punishments, but most of all because they offend You, my God, Who are all good and deserving of all my love. I firmly resolve, with the help of Your grace, to confess my sins, to do penance, and to amend my life. *Amen.*

PRAYER BEFORE MEALS

Bless us O Lord, and these Thy gifts, which we are about to receive, from Thy bounty, through Christ our Lord. *Amen.*

Art Credits

PHOTOGRAPHS:

LINE DRAWINGS, GARY HOFF: